COUNTRIES IN THE NEWS

IRAQ

Kieran Walsh

Rourke

Publishing LLC
Vero Beach, Florida 32964

www.rourkepublishing.com

The country's flag is correct at the time of going to press.

PHOTO CREDITS:
All images © Peter Langer Associated Media Group

Title page: The inner courtyard of a shrine in Baghdad

Editor: Frank Sloan

Cover and interior design by Nicola Stratford

Library of Congress Cataloging-in-Publication Data

Walsh, Kieran.
  Iraq / Kieran Walsh.
     p. cm. — (Countries in the news)
Includes bibliographical references and index.
Contents: Welcome to Iraq — The people — Life in Iraq — School and sports — Food and holidays — The future — Fast facts — The Muslim world.
  ISBN 1-58952-678-3
  1. Iraq—Juvenile literature. [1. Iraq.] I. Title. II. Series.

  DS70.62.W35 2003
  956.7—dc21

                                                        2003005670

Printed in the USA
CG/CG

TABLE OF CONTENTS

WELCOME TO
IRAQ

Iraq is a large country in southwestern Asia. It is located at the northern end of the Persian Gulf. At its widest point Iraq is about 500 miles (800 kilometers) across. The country is slightly larger than the state of California.

There is a flat plain in the center of the country. Iraq has deserts in the west and southwest, and there are mountains in the northeast. Except for the mountains, temperatures are generally warm throughout Iraq.

The shrine of Sheikh Omar Al-Sharawardi in Baghdad.

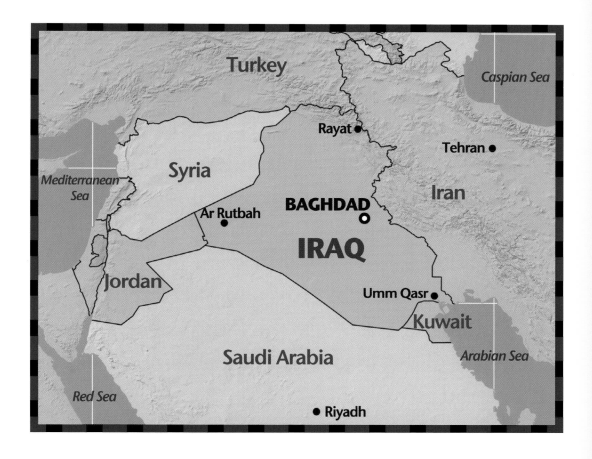

The **Tigris** and **Euphrates** rivers run north to south through Iraq. The soil between the rivers is fertile, which means farming is good.

This land was once known as **Mesopotamia**. This part of Iraq was also once home to the **Sumerians** and then the **Babylonians**.

Iraq became an independent nation in 1932. Before that, the land was under British rule for much of the 20th century.

Baghdad is the capital of Iraq. It is also the country's largest city. It is a blend of the old and the new. There are the famous **bazaars**, but Baghdad is also a bustling and modern industrial city.

Since 1927, when it was discovered, oil has been Iraq's most important product. This large supply of oil has made Iraq a very powerful country. Apart from oil, however, the country does not have many **natural resources**.

A rug seller displays his goods in a typical street bazaar.

THE PEOPLE

People who live in Iraq are known as **Iraqis**. About three quarters of these people are Arabs. About 20 percent of Iraqis are not Arabs. They are known as Kurds. **Kurds** do not always agree with the Iraqi government.

Devout Muslims in the courtyard of a shrine in Baghdad

The Imam Al-Hussein Shrine in Kerbala

Most of the Arabs are **Muslims**, which means they follow the religion of **Islam**. More than half of these Muslims are members of a **sect** known as **Shiites**. About 40 percent of the rest of the Arabs are members of another sect, the **Sunnis**.

Some Iraqis are nomads. This means they wander from place to place, usually in the deserts. These **Bedouin** keep animals, and they spend much of their time looking for food and shelter for their livestock. Marsh Arabs live in the swamps of the south. Most of them fish for a living.

More and more, however, Iraqis are settling in cities, where they can go to find better jobs and permanent homes. Now, about two thirds of Iraqis live in cities.

A nomad herds his camels in the Iraqi desert.

LIFE IN
IRAQ

In cities, people look very much like those in the cities of the United States, for example. There are many cars, which means there is a lot of traffic and noise.

In many Muslim countries, women are brought up to stay at home. In Iraq, however, women have different lives. They are encouraged to go to school and then to look for jobs outside the home. Most Iraqi women do not wear long robes or cover their faces.

A typical street scene in Baghdad

An Iraqi family on the banks of the Tigris River

SCHOOL AND SPORTS

Children are required to go to school in Iraq, and schooling is free. Most people take advantage of schools, and many people in Iraq can read and write. More women go to school than in many Muslim countries.

But in many places there are few schools, and teachers are scarce. More and more colleges and universities are being founded.

Soccer is the number one sport in Iraq. Many people go to stadiums to see soccer games being played, but they also watch it on TV. Other popular sports include basketball, volleyball, weightlifting, wrestling, and boxing.

Some Iraqi schoolchildren dress in modern clothes.

FOOD AND HOLIDAYS

Kebabs of lamb or chicken are popular foods in Iraq. And fish from the Tigris River is another well-liked meal. Popular beverages are strong Arab coffee and hot tea, which is usually served in glasses. For dessert, fruit is often served. So is a pastry known as **baklava**, which is made from ground nuts and honey mixed with thin, crispy dough.

> **!** Iraq's most famous Muslim holiday is **Ramadan**, which is a month-long celebration. During the day, people must fast, but at night they may eat certain foods. When the month is over, Iraqis celebrate at **Id ul Fitr**, when families meet and exchange presents and eat hearty meals.

Vegetables are for sale in this street market.

The Imam Hadi mosque in Samarra

THE FUTURE

Oil brings in almost all of Iraq's foreign income. This means that Iraq should be able to develop industry in the country and to develop other technologies. Roads are needed to connect parts of Iraq, and power stations are needed to bring electricity to many rural villages.

Water is mostly drinkable in the cities, but in the countryside there is a lack of safe drinking water. And, although much of Iraq has enough water for growing crops, some of the country still needs **irrigation** for good farming.

Often, the money from oil has been spent on war and weapons. Iraq's growth in the future depends very much on how the country spends its money.

FAST FACTS

Area: 167,600 square miles
(434,050 square kilometers)

Borders: Jordan, Syria, Turkey,
Iran, Kuwait, Saudi Arabia

Population: 24,001,816
Monetary Unit: dinar

Largest Cities: Baghdad (4,958,000);
Arbil (2,369,000); Basra (1,337,000)
Government: Republic
Religion: Muslim 97%; Shiite Muslim (60-65%);
Sunni Muslim (32-37%)
Crops: grains, dates, cotton
Natural Resources: oil, gas
Major Industries: oils, chemicals,
textiles, construction materials

THE MUSLIM WORLD

There are more than 1,200,000,000 Muslims in the world. Almost two thirds of them live in Asia and Africa. There are two major groups of Muslims: 16% of them are Shiite and 83% are known as Sunni.

Muslims follow the Islam religion. Muslims believe in God, who they know as Allah. The religion was begun around AD 610 when Muhammad became known as a prophet. He wrote down his teachings in a holy book called the Koran.

Muslims are required to pray five times a day. When they do so, they should pray facing Mecca, their holy city. They should also attempt to make a pilgrimage once in their lives to Mecca.

GLOSSARY

Babylonians (BAB uh lone ianz) — an early civilization in Iraq

baklava (back luh VAH) — a pastry made from honey and nuts

bazaars (BUH ZAHRZ) — street markets

Bedouin (BED ooh en) — nomads of the Middle East

Euphrates (you FRAY teez) — one of Iraq's two main rivers

Id ul Fitr (ID UHL FIT ur) — a holiday celebrated at the end
of Ramadan

Iraqis (ear AH kees) — natives of the country of Iraq

irrigation (ir uh GAY shun) — a system that provides water
for crops

Islam (IZ lahm) — the religion followed by Muslims

Kurds (KURDZ) — non Arabic natives of Iraq

Mesopotamia (mess uh pot AY me uh) — a former name for the
land of Iraq

Muslims (MUZ lumz) — people who follow the religion of Islam

natural resources (NAT you ral REE sors ez) — crops or minerals
that occur in a place and that may be valuable to the country

Ramadan (RAM uh DAN) — the ninth month of the Muslim year

sect (SECKT) — a group of people

Shiites (SHEE ITES) — a sect of Muslims, known for being liberal

Sumerians (SOO mehr ee unz) — an ancient civilization of Iraq

Sunnis (SOO NEEZ) — a sect of Muslims, basically conservative

Tigris (TIE grus) — one of Iraq's two main rivers

FURTHER READING

Find out more about Iraq with these helpful books:

- Balcavage, Dinyse. *Iraq.* Gareth Stevens, 2003.
- Marchant, Kerena. *Muslim Festival Tales.* Raintree Steck Vaughn, 2001.
- Stevens, Kathryn. *Iraq.* Child's World, 1999.

WEBSITE TO VISIT

- home.achilles.net/~sal/iraq _history.html

INDEX

About the Author

Kieran Walsh is a writer of children's nonfiction books, primarily on historical and social studies topics. A graduate of Manhattan College, in Riverdale, NY, his degree is in Communications. Walsh has been involved in the children's book field as editor, proofreader, and illustrator as well as author.